Dedicated to anyone who's had a showdown
with a blank sheet of paper... and lost.

STEVE FADIE

Words
to the
Rescue 2:

The sentiment guide
for the tongue tied.

Orange Sky
B O O K S

Indispensable. It has a permanent place on my desk. *Colleen Kilpatrick, Send Out Cards*

Charming book... much needed in today's society. *Clarice Drew, The Clarice Drew Show*

A friend complimented me on my note. I didn't say where I found the inspiration. *Cheryl Poole, education administrator*

The size, length and layout are right on. Fun to read. *Bill Biliti, creative director*

When an office sympathy card came around to sign, I used *Words to the Rescue* to let my co-worker know how sad I was for their loss. *Nancy Doan, financial administrator*

Words to the Rescue helps you let people know that you care. *Kathy Hyink, therapist*

Contents

A vocabulary of truth and simplicity will
be of service throughout your life.
~ Winston Churchill

Introduction

Getting tongue tied seems to be a universal
phenomenon. At least that's what I've observed since
Words to the Rescue was published three years ago.

Yet in today's digital world — with its unending
opportunities for easy personal communications — the
need for fresh, thoughtful words is bigger than ever.
That is the reason for this book.

I'm thrilled that a variety of people find *Words to
the Rescue* useful: from Facebook and Twitter users,
to scrapbook makers and greeting card creators, to
business people and everyday note writers. So much so,
that many of you have asked to be rescued with fresh
new words. I am happy to deliver.

The hardest part of creating a work like this is
deciding what to include in a limited number of
pages. In WTTR 2, you'll find all-new messages for
everyday occasions like Birthdays, Congratulations,
Encouragement and Sympathy. You'll also find messages
for Valentine's Day, Easter, Mother's Day, Father's Day,
Thanksgiving, Christmas and New Year's. In addition,

readers asked for sections on Pregnancy, Engagement and Pet Loss, which are also included.

To make it easier to find what you need quickly, there are more subsections. Finally, a new section, Personality Picks, helps you create a quick note to just about anyone, using complimentary character traits.

Many people ask how I come up with the messages in *Words to the Rescue*. My ear is always poised to pick up on fresh language. I keep 3x5 cards on my desk, on the kitchen counter, in my briefcase and in the car to jot down ideas. I am inspired by TV, radio, the Internet, magazines, newspapers, and people around me. Many of my words come from cards I've written or received. Most come from just sitting down and writing.

From the look of things, there is virtually no limit to the ways readers use *Words to the Rescue*. Friends tell me that writing Birthday, Get Well, Sympathy and other Facebook or Twitter messages is easier when you've got inspiration at your fingertips. Same goes for making your own greeting cards. Or writing a personal note on a greeting card you've purchased. Scrapbookers use the Fast Phrases section to create page titles.

A salesman I heard about keeps the book in his car to help when jotting quick notes. A cake maker was thrilled to find sentiments to write on her cakes. Church ministry members find encouraging words for cards they send to ill or hospitalized parishioners.

When do you turn to *Words to the Rescue*? Write me at steve@WordsToTheRescue.com and let me know. I'd love to hear from you.

However you use these pages, I hope you will be inspired to keep celebrating, thanking and encouraging the special people in your life. Remember, our words can do amazing things.

~ Steve Fadie

1.
Appreciation

> The deepest principle in human nature
> is the craving to be appreciated.
> ~ William James

Neighbor, you rock my city block.

Brightly shines the sun.
But nothing outshines you.

I'll never hesitate to appreciate
how great you rate.

My robust appreciation to <u>the entire staff</u>
for <u>making my stay so comfortable</u>.

To personalize a message, insert your own words where you see <u>underlines</u>.

9

Appreciation

With eternal thanks for your
<u>infinite contributions</u>.

∽

If thank you's were ice cream cones,
I'd be serving you a triple-dipper.

∽

Your <u>thoughtfulness</u>, <u>caring</u> and <u>compassion</u>
<u>lightened our pain</u> during <u>a rough time</u>.

∽

All <u>I've</u> been hearing all this week is
how much everyone loved <u>your speech</u>.
Thanks for <u>energizing our club</u>.

∽

To show <u>our</u> appreciation, <u>we</u> wanted
to hire a quartet of singing monkeys.
But working out the contract was bananas.

Think for a moment... chances are you'll find someone to thank today.

<u>Our</u> appreciation and adulation
for being such a total sensation.

❧

This low-calorie note
contains no sugar-coated words, only
<u>my highest praise</u> for <u>a sweet friend.</u>

❧

<u>Your dad and I</u> are super appreciative
of your positive initiative.

❧

Your roll-up-your-sleeves dedication
to <u>the Westwood community</u> inspires
us deeply. Thank you, <u>Sean.</u>

❧

Prayers have been answered. Dreams have come
true. There's only one person to blame: YOU.

It costs nothing to write a note of appreciation. But the value is priceless.

EMPLOYEE

Standing O!

～

My gratitude to a proactive <u>guy</u>
who provides solutions before
I even know there are problems.

～

Double thanks for:
1. Doing the job.
2. Doing it right.

～

Thank you, <u>Julie</u>, for the friendly way you
<u>make clients feel welcome in our office.</u>

～

<u>We're</u> singing the praises of the <u>man</u> who
<u>keeps our department humming</u> every day.

Your sincere thanks encourages employees to repeat positive behavior.

EMPLOYEE

You're one in two million.

∽

Your <u>creative contributions</u> this year
have been a shining example for all of us.

∽

For a small business like ours to succeed,
we depend on people with big talents.
Thanks for joining us.

∽

You possess the rare talent to be a
circus superstar. The way you juggle
all the jobs around here is <u>amazing</u>.

∽

<u>Multi-talented</u>. <u>Outstanding</u>. <u>Sharp</u>.
These are the words that come up
whenever your name comes up.

For more inspiration, see page 143 for a list of positive character traits.

MILITARY

Bravely, honorably and selflessly you
<u>serve/served</u>. Deeply, sincerely and
gratefully, we thank you.

∾

You may not know it, but you have a fan club.
Can you hear the thunderous applause?

∾

Red, white and blue wishes of
appreciation for all you do, every day,
to help preserve our American way of life.

∾

You know we love you, <u>Uncle Jack</u>.
We also want you to know we respect you
for serving <u>in Iraq</u>.

∾

Honoring your personal sacrifice in the
defense of our country's freedom.

Thank a soldier or veteran. We owe each one a mountain of gratitude.

words to the resue } Appreciation

MILITARY

Here's to you, soldier.

∽

From ordinary Americans to
extraordinary ones: Peace and Godspeed.
Safe journey home.

∽

With hearts of gratitude, we honor
you, and everyone who has buttoned on
the military uniform of the USA.

∽

Being in the military requires <u>physical
stamina</u>, <u>mental toughness</u> and <u>courage</u>. You
know, a high-caliber individual like you.

∽

Freedom is a breath of night air, a road paved
with possibilities, an eagle soaring overhead.
Freedom is a gift, given by people like you.

Send a care package to a soldier. Find out how at www.anysoldier.com.

TEACHER

My brain needed a kick-start.
Your class was premium fuel.

∽

Teaching our kids to become
intelligent citizens is one of life's
most esteemed callings.

∽

Big Bird is yellow. Kermit is green. You are the
<u>best</u> <u>pre-school teacher</u> we've ever seen.

∽

And the award for best teacher in a supporting
role goes to <u>Miss Arnold</u>. Bravo.

∽

You're as good as it gets, <u>Mr. Brown</u>. Thank
goodness you were <u>my teacher</u> this year.

A note of appreciation is a gift in itself. Write one today.

words to the rescue } Appreciation

TEACHER

<u>Mrs. Bell:</u> Your class
gives wings to my imagination.

∽

If teaching is an art,
you're one of the masters.

∽

As parents of <u>three elementary students</u>,
we are awed by your <u>passion for teaching</u>.
Thank you for <u>an exceptional year</u>.

∽

You pushed. You prodded. You challenged
us to be our best. There's just one thing
we wish for you this summer. Rest.

∽

Is there any way we can clone you, <u>Mr.
Santana</u>? The world needs <u>teachers</u> like you.

Why wait until the end of the school year to thank your favorite educator?

TEACHER

Grade-A teachers are rare.
Thanks for being one.

❧

My brain is bigger, faster
and stronger because of you.

❧

Lucky, lucky me to have
a <u>principal</u> as <u>nice</u> as you.

❧

Another year, another crop
of <u>bright, shining young people</u>
ready to <u>energize the world</u>.

❧

<u>Coach Miller</u>: You showed us
<u>the meaning of teamwork</u>. But mostly,
you helped us <u>become better people</u>.

Let the words on this page inspire you to write words of your own.

TEACHER

The lessons you taught us
didn't end in class.

❦

Note to <u>Fearless Leader</u>:
Thanks for instilling in us the
courage to always keep trying.

❦

Kudos to everyone at
<u>St. Paul's Academy</u>. Nobody's
better at <u>firing up young souls</u>.

❦

To say you're a class act, <u>Mr. Johnson</u>, is
the oldest pun in the book. But it's true.

❦

To our multi-talented <u>orchestra teacher</u>,
who's been instrumental in making
this year <u>monumental</u>.

There are thousands of ways to say thank you. Fortunately, you only need one.

⸭ Appreciation

VOLUNTEER

Of course we appreciate your time.
Even more, we appreciate you.

❧

Thanks to our <u>big league</u>
volunteers. When a job needs doing,
you always <u>step up to the plate</u>.

❧

Without you, we'd be up a creek
without a paddle... and sinking fast.

❧

The <u>neighbors</u> thank you. The
<u>flower beds</u> thank you. A garden of
thanks for <u>beautifying Grant Street</u>.

❧

You contribute something
special to everything you do.
We warmly and gratefully thank you.

Words of thanks are words of gold.

Appreciation

VOLUNTEER

You're as good as it gets.
Thank goodness you're on our team.

❧

Cheers to our volunteers...
you keep us smiling year after year.

❧

Volunteers are the glue that
holds the Sante Fe Women's Club
together. Thanks for sticking with us.

❧

Without generous, and faith-filled
folks like you, we'd never be able to
spread the good news to so many.

❧

We are beholden to you. Not just today,
but as long as Valley Hospital continues
providing healing care to our community.

Stage actors thrive on applause. Volunteers thrive on your thanks.

words to the rescue 〉 Appreciation

VOLUNTEER

You've earned
something money can't buy.
Our admiration.

∽

Hey, Mr. Unbelievably Talented:
Thanks for sharing.

∽

Your passion for serving others is
not only commendable. It's inspirational.

∽

It gives me great pleasure to recognize your
compassionate service, day-in and day-out,
as we create a better hospice.

∽

You have our deepest thanks for your
exemplary leadership at the Helping Network.

Your appreciation is highly valued compensation to a volunteer.

2.
Birthday

Everyone is the age of their heart.
~ Guatemalan proverb

It's your day. Embrace
your inner cupcake.

Another year older?
Banish the thought.

If there's still hope for <u>me</u>,
there's plenty left for you.

No way is <u>42</u> old. Think of yourself
as <u>28</u> with <u>14</u> years experience.

To personalize a message, insert your own words where <u>underlines</u> appear.

TO HIM

Birthday props, pops.

❧

Whoop de do, dude.
It's your birthday.

❧

Birthdays don't matter.
<u>Beer</u> does.

❧

<u>Guys</u> like you have an advantage.
You just keep getting more
<u>distinguished</u> every year.

❧

Best wishes to the guy with <u>a</u>
<u>wonderful life</u> (and a horrible <u>golf game</u>).

Add a laugh to your birthday wishes; share a riddle or joke.

words to the rescue } **Birthday**

TO HIM

Birthday kisses to my
highly valued antique.

⌒⌒

You may be younger,
but I've got you beat when
it comes to <u>medical procedures</u>.

⌒⌒

If you were a maple tree,
I'd sing you Sappy Birthday.

⌒⌒

Welcome to the Middle Ages, sir.

⌒⌒

As we climb the ladder of birthday
bliss, life's deeper questions arise.
Like, "<u>Where did I put the car keys?</u>"

Spouse's birthday? Check the Romance & Fun section, page 69.

TO HER

Birthdays are for paupers.
We royals never age.

⌒

Age is only a number.
Around here, we don't do numbers.

⌒

When one arrives at our level
of refinement, one stops counting
pitiful little things like birthdays.

⌒

Inquiring minds want to know:
What's your secret for looking
<u>ten years</u> younger than you are?

⌒

Just because you're a tiny bit older doesn't
mean you have to give up <u>pole dancing</u>.

For more Birthday ideas, see Fast Phrases, page 132.

TO HER

Remember, it's all
about the frosting.

❦

Birthday madness to
<u>my</u> favorite <u>mama</u>.

❦

Happy birthday to the
<u>fashionable lady</u> who proves: <u>The
higher the hair, the closer to God.</u>

❦

What the <u>queen</u> wants, the <u>queen</u> gets.
Happy birthday, <u>your majesty</u>.

❦

You have the right to remain fabulous.
Anything you say or do may be used as
evidence of your greatness.

Remember the good times. Share a memory with the birthday girl.

ADVENTURES IN AGING

Hee... hee... hee... you're older than me.
(But who's counting?)

∽

You're only young once. And if you work
it right, once is enough.
~ Joe E. Lewis

∽

More birthdays = more fabulous.

∽

You've earned the right to stop
counting birthdays. There are more
important things to track, like grandkids.

∽

There's not much good to say about
getting older. Unless you consider
the senior discount at Old Country Buffet.

What trait do you most admire about the birthday person? Share with them.

ADVENTURES IN AGING

Your age is only one part of you.
(In this case, a big part.)

∽◌

Too old for <u>break dancing</u>.
Too young for <u>shuffleboard</u>.

∽◌

Affirmations for contented aging:
1. Wrinkles are a hoot. 2. Weight is
just a number. 3. Gravity is a happy thing.

∽◌

Some say with age the brain
gets like mashed potatoes.
If true, please pass the gravy.

∽◌

Relax, friend. It takes until <u>40</u>
to <u>learn who you are</u>. And <u>ten more years</u>
to <u>feel comfortable with it</u>.

Post your clever birthday wish on Facebook for all to see.

ADVENTURES IN AGING

Geesh.
And I thought I was old.

⤳

Winter is on my head.
But spring is in my heart.
~Victor Hugo

⤳

Hey... not fair.
You're aging backwards.

⤳

Your obvious specialty:
Aging gracefully.

⤳

It's sad to grow old, but nice to ripen.
~Brigitte Bardot

Birthdays aren't always happy. Tell them you understand their hard times.

FRIEND

Stay gorgeous,
gorgeous.

❧

An <u>exceptional</u> birthday to
an <u>exceptional</u> <u>coworker</u>.

❧

<u>Forty</u>. Fierce. And Fantastic.
[Also use 14, 24, 34, etc.]

❧

Forever young,
forever fabulous.

❧

You still have "it"
and always will.

On their birthdays, thank family members for their love and support.

FRIEND

<u>Thirty-four</u>, huh?
Been there... done that.

❧

<u>Wacky</u> birthday wishes from
your much younger friend.

❧

Here's to life
in the Fab Lane.

❧

One day you and I will be old.
Not.

❧

Forget about getting older.
Aging is stricty for cheese.

Surprise an old friend you haven't talked to in years. Send a birthday card.

FRIEND

I smell candles.
Lots and lots of candles.

❧

Bodacious birthday wishes,
young lady.

❧

To high-flying adventures,
for old <u>wind bags</u> like us.

❧

What fountain of youth
are you sipping from?

❧

Hugs and happy days
to my <u>kind</u>, <u>thoughtful</u>, and
<u>understanding</u> birthday <u>friend</u>.

Dig up an old photo of you and a friend and share it in a note, card or email.

words to the rescue ⟩ **Birthday**

KIDS

Birthday hugs
to my cake-smashing cutie.

⌒

Although you've grown up like a weed,
you're a bright, happy sunflower to
<u>your proud parents.</u>

⌒

Sprinkles, tickles and giggles
to <u>the birthday baby.</u>

⌒

No matter how you spell it, <u>Dana,</u>
you're one fantastic niece:
<u>Divine. Artistic. Neat. Athletic.</u>

⌒

Hey <u>Q-T-Pie:</u> You're the apple of my eye.

Share a joke with your favorite kid on their birthday. See page 66.

KIDS

To a bling-a-licious birthday.

∽◌

As your <u>grandparents,</u> it is our duty
to spoil you on your birthday.

∽◌

I refuse to believe you are
<u>a teenager</u> already. Say it ain't so.

∽◌

Love and hugs to <u>the smart young lady</u> who
is now <u>16</u>. Keep moving... keep
reaching... and keep <u>your room clean</u>.

∽◌

I was going to write you a rap song
to celebrate your birthday.
But I ran out of wrapping paper.

Kids thrive on encouragement. Put yours in writing on a birthday card.

KIDS

My favorite thing in the world
isn't a thing. It's you.

෧෧

Happy Birthday to my one-of-a-kind
nephew <u>Justin</u>: <u>Joyful. Unique. Sportsman.
Talented. Inventive. Nice.</u>

෧෧

When God sent you to <u>dance for us</u>, our
<u>darling diva</u>, he gave us the best gift.

෧෧

Time for presents. Time for fun.
Time to celebrate the <u>fantastic</u> one!

෧෧

<u>Trevor</u>: In all of history there will never
be another <u>awesome dude</u> exactly like you.

There's nothing like getting a birthday card in the mail. Kids love it.

3.
Congratulations

By sharing in the happiness of others,
we add to our own.
~ Author Unknown

Well la-dee-da!

Awesome is as
awesome does.

I'm so thrilled for you,
I could do 12 back handsprings.
(If only my spine would cooperate).

The universe is giving you
a big thumbs up. We echo the sentiment.

To personalize a message, insert your own words where underlines appear.

ACHIEVEMENT

Congratulations to the <u>queen of determination</u>.

∽

Look... it's raining champagne.

∽

You're in the winner's circle.
I'm in awe.

∽

What once seemed like
"mission impossible" is now
"mission achievable."

∽

There's nothing to like about
putting on a tux. But I'll do anything to
support <u>my #1 on her special day</u>.

When you affirm positive behavior, it encourages a person to repeat it.

Congratulations

ACHIEVEMENT

Nicely done,
artistic one.

∾

Hey Ace: nice work.

∾

Sha-ZAM you nailed it.

∾

We totally enjoyed your play.
(Especially the scenes you were in.)
The vocals, choreography and
acting were Broadway all the way.

∾

You've reminded us once again,
that with <u>focus and determination</u>,
just about anything is possible.

Celebrate their special achievement. Tell them how proud you are.

ADOPTION

A dream come true...
and nobody deserves it more than you.

࿇

With grateful hearts and
outstretched arms, we warmly welcome
<u>Lucas</u> to the <u>Johannas family</u>.

࿇

No matter what. No matter how.
Love always finds a way... as
<u>you and Melissa</u> have proven.

࿇

You haven't just added a son to the
family. You've added a shining sun.

࿇

Your <u>new daughter Jessica</u> is fortunate to
be chosen and loved by two standout parents.

There is no love like that of the parent for the child. –Henry Ward Beecher

words to the rescue ⎰ Congratulations

BABY

And baby makes three.

∽

A new life in its infancy, a new
branch on the <u>Jackson</u> family tree.

∽

When a child is born, so is a grandpa.
~ Italian proverb

∽

Savor every minute of
silly baby giggles. (You'll need to
save some laughs for the teen years.)

∽

Since the dawn of civilization, human beings
have asked "What's life all about?" Now,
as you cradle your newborn, you know.

A birth is a milestone. Mark the event with a personal note.

⟩ Congratulations

BABY

Happy snuggles,
cuddles and giggles.

✧

This <u>lad</u> is destined for
<u>greatness</u>. Just look at how
<u>phenomenal</u> his <u>uncle</u> is.

✧

Joy to the world! And especially
to the two <u>beaming</u> parents.

✧

You're going to have to learn a new
language. Don't worry. You'll pick up
the ga-ga goo-goo routine in no time.

✧

From cute baby nose to soft baby toes,
your new <u>son</u> is a head-to-foot miracle.

Give baby a personalized blanket with your embroidered dedication.

ENGAGEMENT

I'm thrilled. I'm elated.
Let's get inebriated.

∽

Fantastically fantastic. Wonderfully
wonderful. Awesomely awesome.

∽

The best tears are
happy tears. Mine have been flowing
like a river <u>since hearing your good news</u>.

∽

It's good to see two young
hearts joining together. (Especially
since you'll be saving so much on taxes.)

∽

When I heard that you were engaged, the
first thing I did was fall to my knees,
look up to heaven and exclaim: It's about time!

For more inspiration, see Fast Phrases, page 133.

ENGAGEMENT

Happy ball and chain.

∽

And they loved
happily ever after.

∽

Happiness is having an MVP:
Most Valued Partner.

∽

Here's to infinite years
of love, laughter and light.

∽

How do <u>we</u> know this
<u>young lady</u> of yours is <u>so special</u>?
Because that's the way <u>we've</u>
always thought of you.

If you're enjoying this book, chances are your friends will too. See page 150.

ENGAGEMENT

Our kudos and congrats
to a perfect pair.

∽

The universe has brought
the two of you together for a reason.

∽

We're thrilled and excited for you.
Keep the flame burning.

∽

What a blessing to find the right <u>man</u>.
Now if you can find the right <u>dress</u>
you'll be all set.

∽

Sharing life with the one you love
is one of life's true joys. (<u>Dirty socks
on the floor?</u> You'll get over it.)

Give the new couple a note with your personal tips for a happy marriage.

⟨ # Congratulations

PREGNANCY

Life, liberty and the pursuit
of parenthood.

∽

From here to maternity...
enjoy your pregnancy.

∽

Good things come to those who mate.
(As you and <u>Max</u> have proven.)

∽

Crib note: Heard you'll soon
be adding a new bed to your home,
and a little <u>bambino</u> to go with it.

∽

Congratulations on your
newest project under construction.

Share your pregnancy story with the mom-to-be. "I'll never forget when..."

RETIREMENT

It won't be the same around here
without you. (Finally, some sanity.)

❧

Now's your chance
to color outside the lines.

❧

You retire? That's like
asking a bear to give up honey.

❧

The "R" word doesn't apply
to you. Let's just call this new phase
of your life "adjusting the schedule."

❧

Retirement duties:
1. Walk dog. 2. Stay out of wife's way.

Retirement is a major life change. Your words can help smooth the transition.

RETIREMENT

Way to go, you young
whippersnapper you.

❧

Happy unexpected discoveries.
Happy creative adventures.
Happy new phase of your life.

❧

Heck yes we're going
to miss you. If we ever stop
fighting over who gets <u>your office</u>.

❧

Finally, your chance to do
whatever you want, whenever you
want. Just don't forget to <u>sleep</u>.

❧

Re-tire is what you do to a car.
What you're doing is re-invigorating.

Write a note telling the retiree how much you enjoyed working with them.

4.
Encouragement

It is not the mountain we conquer
but ourselves.
~ Edmund Hillary

Hang tough.
This shall pass.

Hugger-oonies to you, <u>sis</u>.

Every wall is a door.
~ Ralph Waldo Emerson

God has his hand on your back.

I'm your <u>mother</u>. When you hurt,
I hurt. When you cry, I cry.

To personalize a message, insert your own words where <u>underlines</u> appear.

CANCER SUPPORT

You may have <u>cancer</u>.
But <u>cancer</u> doesn't have you.

❧

As your friend of <u>23</u> years,
I know you well. I also know you
possess the strength to <u>get through this</u>.

❧

Cancer sucks. I wish I could turn back the
hands of time and take away your diagnosis.

❧

We know how stressed you
must be. Doctors, medications,
appointments and tests can wear you down.

❧

Many people are rallying for you, your
<u>friends and family</u> who love you as we do.

A cancer patient needs your support right now. Send a note just to say "hi."

CANCER SUPPORT

You survived <u>that mullet haircut</u>.
You can survive anything.

∽

Even if all you want to do is scream,
call me. I'm very good at it.
(We'll see who can yell loudest.)

∽

Now that the worst is behind you,
I recommend some good healthy
<u>fishing/shopping</u>.

∽

Praying, wishing, hoping, crossing our
fingers and toes for you...

∽

Help! I'm drowning. My frontal cortex is
flooded with thoughts of you.

Although cancer is scary, a little humor can be very healthy.

DISAPPOINTMENT

No matter how <u>broken, bruised,</u>
<u>or defeated</u> you feel, I'll always have
a <u>chocolate cupcake</u> waiting for you.

∞

You didn't need <u>to win the pageant</u>,
<u>Sarah</u>, to be a winner in <u>my</u> book.

∞

<u>Your father and I</u> are heartsick
over your <u>streak of bad luck</u>.

∞

Life can be tangled and confusing.
The good news is, you possess the
natural ability to figure anything out.

∞

I'm sorry you didn't <u>make the cut, Kyle</u>.
There are more important things ahead.
Like a <u>steak dinner Saturday night</u>.

Life has both mountains and valleys. Show your support during the low times.

Encouragement

DISAPPOINTMENT

This is only a temporary setback
You'll soon be back on track speeding ahead
faster than a bullet train.

❧

You've become a stronger person because
of the challenges you've been through.

❧

Now and then, life sucks. You've proven
you're a fighter, <u>Jack.</u> Keep punching.

❧

When you feel the weight of the world
on your shoulders, remember: You have
something others don't - our support.

❧

Abraham is said to have been 100
when son Isaac was born.
Divine proof... anything is possible.

Three simple words from you can help them keep going. "Hang in there."

Encouragement

DIVORCE / SPLIT-UP

New life.
New singlehood. New horizons.

❦

Like a dove escaping from
its cage, may your <u>suffering</u> fly away.

❦

You deserve credit for
getting through as painful a
situation as life can serve up.

❦

Remember: Every morning brings a
sunrise. But even better... <u>donuts</u>.

❦

Keep in mind <u>Cindy</u>: Those
who do you wrong have no power to
determine your happiness. Only you do.

Divorce is painful. Your words can be a blanket of comfort.

DIVORCE / SPLIT-UP

There is no medicine for a
broken heart. (Except maybe the mall.)

⚬⟋⚬

It's OK to be sad.
Anyone who's been through
what you have, would feel the same.

⚬⟋⚬

I believe there's a girl out there
who can give you everything you
deserve... in other words, the best.

⚬⟋⚬

Keep up your Steel Magnolia spirit.
It's served you beautifully throughout life.

⚬⟋⚬

You've been through the grinder
yet still maintained a positive attitude.
That says a lot about your personal fortitude.

Do you know somebody who is starting over? Offer your encouragement.

Encouragement

PEP TALK

Hey, you're in good company.
Picasso had a blue period too.

⁓

Not until we are lost
do we begin to find ourselves.
~ Henry David Thoreau

⁓

Respect God, do what is right,
and you will walk unafraid.
~ Norman Vincent Peale

⁓

There is only one success, to be able to
spend your life in your own way.
~ Christopher Morley

⁓

Opportunities multiply as they are seized.
~ Sun Tzu

Give a personal gift that costs nothing - encouraging words.

words to the rescue } # Encouragement

PEP TALK

We cannot direct the wind.
But we can adjust the sails.
~ Author unknown

❧

<u>Jim</u>: You have a mountain of gold
within you. Keep digging.

❧

You can do anything you set your mind to,
and you can do it in stilettos.
~ Kimora Lee Simmons

❧

Whenever you doubt your talents,
remember... all masterpieces start as
a work in progress. Then keep going.

❧

No matter how tough things get, you can
take positive steps to improve your life.

Today, send a surprise note to someone who needs a boost.

Encouragement

WEIGHT LOSS

Every pound lost...
a bushel of willpower gained.

∽

Your determination to get
in shape is admirable, <u>Admiral</u>.

∽

Believe in yourself and
your abilities. Your family does.

∽

Do any of us really need a
<u>jelly-filled donut</u>? Eating right
is the best revenge. Keep it up.

∽

Our kids deserve a <u>healthy dad.</u>
Watching you take positive steps to <u>lose</u>
<u>weight</u> makes my heart <u>swell with pride.</u>

Losing weight can be a struggle. Affirm their positive steps with a note.

Encouragement

WEIGHT LOSS

Whoohooo. Look at you.

❧

Forget the pat of butter.
You deserve a pat on the back.

❧

No matter what the scale says,
my love for you will always
come supersized.

❧

I don't know if you've noticed...
but you're becoming the new,
improved version of yourself: Greg 2.0.

❧

You are more powerful than a
cheeseburger and fries... stronger
than a bowl of chocolate fudge ice cream.

Your positive words can help fuel their journey to success.

WEIGHT LOSS

You CAN do this.

❧

With your love of life
and passion for helping others,
you deserve to succeed.

❧

Looking good. Looking hot.
Show the world what you've got.

❧

Every journey
begins with a single step.
Congratulations on starting yours.

❧

Your gusto for living a
healthier life is contagious.
Where do I sign up?

Your words of support can help a friend through difficult times.

5.
Get Well

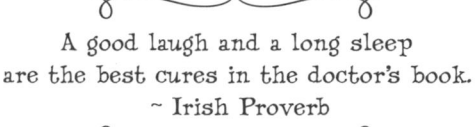

A good laugh and a long sleep
are the best cures in the doctor's book.
~ Irish Proverb

Take care. Take comfort.
Take it day by day.

Your coffee cup is
growing mold... hurry back.

Doctors say a glass of red wine
daily is good for the heart. (Finally
a medicine container with a cork.)

We've all been worrying about you so much,
we're running out of fingernails to bite.

To personalize a message, insert your own words where <u>underlines</u> appear.

My cat <u>Tracer</u>
sends <u>her</u> purrrrrs.

❧

<u>We</u> so much want you
to bounce back to health.

❧

Hope your recovery is like
a vitamin-packed cereal: TOTAL.

❧

Get your butt out of that bed
immediately, <u>Alexa</u>... or I'll march over
in my <u>iron-toed boots</u> and <u>kick you out</u>.

❧

It's vital to view life from a
glass-is-half-full perspective. (We all
need something to wash down our meds.)

See Fast Phrases, page 138 for more Get Well ideas.

Somehow... some way...
we're going to get you better.

⌒⌒

If life had a fast-forward button,
<u>we'd</u> push it now. That way you could
skip the painful part and be back to 100%.

⌒⌒

<u>I've</u> been thinking of you so much,
my brain is threatening to go on strike.

⌒⌒

Broken bones are no fun. But you sure are.
<u>We</u> miss your <u>insane jokes</u>.

⌒⌒

<u>We all</u> hope you're soon <u>back in the saddle</u>.
The <u>accounting department</u> is operating
at <u>a slow gallop</u> without you.

When we're ill, we can feel isolated and alone. Your note can be a lifeline.

CARE / CONCERN

Holding you close in our thoughts.

⚬⟋⚬

Sunshine days and restful nights
to you, Mrs. Jansen, one of the
warmest ladies I've ever known.

⚬⟋⚬

Fondly recalling the fun we shared
so many summers together at the lake.

⚬⟋⚬

Although we've not met, please know
I join many others in asking God's
blessings as you prepare for your surgery.

⚬⟋⚬

This message comes from the heart, from
folks who want you to know you are loved.

Don't know what to say on the card? Just say "Hi... thinking of you."

Get Well

CARE / CONCERN

If prayers were <u>flowers</u>, you'd be
surrounded by <u>a field of daisies</u>.

≈

If there is power in prayer, our healing
petitions for you would light up <u>Times Square</u>.

≈

No day passes when <u>we</u> don't think
of you. Fondly. And with tremendous love.

≈

May the fact that others care, even folks you
don't know, strengthen your spirit this day.

≈

Asking God to richly bless <u>your family,
friends, doctors, nurses and health support
team</u> as they lovingly care for you.

Who needs to hear from you today?

words to the rescue ⟩ **Get Well**

THE LIGHTER SIDE

I want you to smile today. So I've collected
a few jokes to tickle your funny bone.
[Assemble from jokes on these two pages]

∾

What do fish say when
they hit a concrete wall? (Dam!)

∾

How do crazy folks go through the forest?
(They take the psycho path.)

∾

What happened to the cat who
swallowed a ball of yarn? (She had mittens.)

∾

What do you get when you cross a snowman
with a vampire? (Frostbite.)

Laughing is healthy. Send a joke and give them a chuckle.

words to the rescue ⟩ **Get Well**

THE LIGHTER SIDE

Why was the broom late?
(It over swept.)

❧

How did the patient get to
the hospital so fast? (He flu.)

❧

What do you call a short
psychic who escaped from jail?
(A small medium at large.)

❧

What did one eye say to the other?
(Something between us smells.)

❧

What did the hat say to the necklace?
(You hang on and I'll go on ahead.)

There are dozens of online joke sites. Check them out.

words to the rescue ⸮ Get Well

FAMILY SUPPORT

You've earned your angel wings,
caring for <u>your mom</u> so <u>lovingly</u>.

⌁

These days must be extremely
stressful for you <u>and your family</u>.
Please know you are close in our thoughts.

⌁

<u>We're</u> so sorry for the pain your family has
had to endure. It makes <u>us</u> angry that a
person could <u>be so cruel</u> to <u>your daughter</u>.

⌁

Julie: Everyone at <u>Mason Valley School</u>
is rooting for <u>your son</u>, <u>Martin</u>.

⌁

Life can get you down. Way down. Stay strong
and keep your head up. You will survive.

For more ideas, check the Encouragement section, page 49.

6.
Romance & Fun

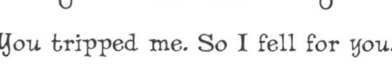

You tripped me. So I fell for you.
~ Author Unknown

From your heart to mine
there is no distance.

Your eyes are hypnotic.
Your body makes me neurotic.

If we were together <u>150</u> years
it wouldn't be enough.

Hey thunder: How about we get together
and make a storm? Love, lightning.

To personalize a message, insert your own words where <u>underlines</u> appear.

words to the rescue { # Romance & Fun

Hello, cupcake.

⤸

A heart you've captured
is totally enraptured.

⤸

I never knew what I wanted
out of life. Then we met
and everything changed.

⤸

Who knows where life will take us next?
<u>Mozambique... Tokyo... Miller's Ice Cream
store on the corner</u>?

⤸

In honor of the Chinese who invented
fireworks, let's get some <u>Moo Goo Gai Pan</u>
and make some sparks of our own.

For more inspiration, check out the Valentine's Day chapter, page 93.

Loving you more each day.

～

Married <u>38</u> years and
still <u>ga-ga goo-goo</u> over you.

～

I don't know if I can make you
as happy as you deserve to be.
But I sure hope you'll let me try.

～

All I ever wanted was someone
to share <u>my scary dreams with in
the morning</u>. How lucky I have you.

～

I was never good at chemistry.
But whatever we have,
I'm totally good with.

Don't have a note card handy? Write on a napkin. It's the thought that counts.

Romance & Fun

Can a person die
of over-excitement?

❦

I can't even begin to tell you
all the things I like about you,
because it's pretty much everything.

❦

Huggable. Smoochable. Unbeatable.
That's you.

❦

I'm just a <u>dopey guy</u> with <u>big feet</u>
who happens to <u>adore</u> you.

❦

I'm happy and excited and giddy
and joyful and nervous... all of that
good stuff rolled into one.

To strengthen your relationship, write short notes to her/him weekly.

7.
Sympathy

We will remember him fondly.

⌒

Losing <u>your beloved mate</u>
<u>of so many years</u> must be
extremely painful.

⌒

<u>Margaret</u> often talked about
<u>her</u> family. It was obvious she was a
<u>caring mother</u> to <u>Brianna and Justin.</u>

⌒

Forever in <u>our</u> hearts... never forgotten.

To personalize a message, insert your own words where <u>underlines</u> appear.

Sympathy

His spirit was so large,
even death cannot defeat him.

∽

A role model and mentor to
thousands of kids, Mr. Groves touched
our lives in a way nobody else could.

∽

With admiration and appreciation,
we say goodbye to a leader
who showed us how to live a good life.

∽

Some are born with blue eyes, some with
red hair. Beth was born with a gold heart.

∽

When remembering Lana, I think of these
qualities: loving, energetic, supportive.

Tell the family what your coworker meant to you. They will appreciate it.

LOSS OF CHILD

Your tragedy has us
heartbroken beyond words.

∽

When the pain is too much,
the tears too big, and the hurt
too deep, you can always lean on <u>us</u>.

∽

Saying goodbye to <u>Morgan</u>, our hearts ache.
Remembering <u>the joy of knowing her</u>,
even for a short time, we are uplifted.

∽

Every life suffers loss.
But your loss is especially painful.

∽

The loss of your <u>cherished
baby daughter Angela</u> must be devastating.
Our most heartfelt sympathies.

Your short note makes a sympathy card even more comforting.

LOSS OF COWORKER / FRIEND

Many people are mourning the loss
of a <u>talented associate and friend</u>.

❦

Our grief is deeply felt because of
how much we <u>cherished</u> Alina, not
just as a <u>coworker</u> but also a <u>friend</u>.

❦

It's hard to find the words to express how
highly we thought of <u>your husband</u> <u>Nick</u>.

❦

We cared deeply about <u>Jaysa</u>. During
these difficult days, please know all of us
at <u>Smith Optical</u> care about you too.

❦

The thing about <u>Jim</u> was he had
this <u>great soul</u> and a <u>huge heart</u>. That was
obvious to everyone at <u>Lake Shore Insurance</u>.

The Thinking of You section, page 89, may also be helpful.

LOSS OF PARENT

In tribute to the <u>woman</u>
who gave you life.

⌒∾

With <u>friendship</u> and <u>love</u>
in the loss of your <u>father</u>.

⌒∾

<u>A hug</u> from your <u>mom</u> made me
feel <u>warm and loved</u>. I will sorely
miss <u>her life-affirming embraces</u>.

⌒∾

Losing a <u>parent</u> is one of the most
painful parts of life. I liked your <u>father</u>
very much and will dearly miss <u>him</u>.

⌒∾

Your <u>father</u> helped make you the wonderful
<u>friend</u> you are today. We salute and honor <u>him</u>.

Losing a parent can hurt deeply. Your caring note helps the grieving process.

PET LOSS

God so loved dogs, he spelled
his name backwards for them.

⌇

The word "pet" didn't apply
to <u>Samantha</u>. She was family.

⌇

From one <u>cat fanatic</u> to another,
my sympathy on the loss of your
friend <u>Murphy</u>.

⌇

Having to come home from the vet
without <u>Sparkles</u> must have been
heartbreaking. I'm crying with you.

⌇

Of all the <u>little black Poodles</u> in the
world, your <u>Pedro</u> had to be the <u>best</u>.

Acknowledging the loss of a pet gives comfort to a person in pain.

PET LOSS

Doggy heaven just gained
another recruit.

❧

T-Rex was one classy canine.
I will miss the way he licked my face.

❧

The strong bond between you and
Boomer was obvious. Although he's
not here, his spirit always will be.

❧

Like seasons, every life has a
beginning and an end. Taco's was
way too short. I'm so sorry.

❧

What an honor to share our lives with
majestic equine companions like Sasha.

For some people, losing a pet is just like losing a family member.

words to the rescue } ## Sympathy

PET LOSS

Fondly remembering <u>Shadow</u>.
Friend. Protector. Companion.

❧

<u>You</u> will surely miss <u>Rex's</u>
movements and heartbeats in the
house. I'm thinking of you.

❧

<u>Our</u> condolences on your
loss of <u>Molly</u>. It's never easy
saying goodbye to a <u>good friend</u>.

❧

<u>You</u> gave <u>Chloe</u> a happy life.
I can see <u>her</u> now... perched on a
puffy white cloud, <u>hugging her cat nip</u>.

❧

From the day <u>you adopted</u> <u>Max</u>, it was
clear <u>he</u> would be <u>a loyal hunting buddy</u>.

Every personal note makes a difference to someone who is grieving.

8.
Thank You

Feeling gratitude and not expressing it
is like wrapping a present and not giving it.
~ William Arthur Ward

In every life,
a little lunacy must fall.
Thanks for being mine.

I am eternally grateful for
<u>your caring and generosity</u>.

I thank <u>my lucky stars</u>, <u>the academy</u>,
and <u>my second grade teacher</u>.
Most of all, I thank you.

Your note is safely stored in my heart.

To personalize a message, insert your own words where <u>underlines</u> appear.

GIFT

[For cookies/cake/bread]
Thanks for baking me so happy.

✑

Then what to <u>my</u> wondering eyes
doth appear, a present from you!

✑

Opening your package and finding <u>so many</u>
<u>gifts,</u> <u>I</u> felt <u>I</u> was being given a huge hug.

✑

The beautiful flowers you sent are
like a mini-vacation. <u>I</u> feel as if <u>I'm</u>
<u>on a sun-drenched Caribbean Island.</u>

✑

It boosted <u>our</u> spirits to open your
thoughtful gift. <u>We'll</u> think of <u>Mom</u> every
time <u>the wind stirs the harmonic chimes.</u>

Keep a supply of note cards and stamps in your briefcase or purse.

Thank You

GIFT

I'm tickled, touched
and totally in awe.

✑

Clouds dance in the sky.
Gratitude dances in my heart.

✑

Like a river, my appreciation flows.
Thank you.

✑

Your gift was the nicest pleasantry
and the most pleasant nicety.

✑

There was one thing
I didn't think of for my new truck.
Thanks for the naked lady mud flaps.

Think of a person from your past who has been a help in your life. Write to them.

Thank You

HOSPITALITY

Thanks for putting <u>us</u> up...
and for putting up with <u>us</u>.

❧

Springtime in <u>Boston</u> is awesome.
So was your <u>dinner party</u>.

❧

A bouquet of thanks to <u>our most
welcoming host and hostess</u>.

❧

The <u>food</u>... the <u>friends</u>... the <u>fish stories</u>...
Your parties are <u>the bomb</u>.

❧

From the <u>personal welcome sign on the door</u>,
to the <u>fresh daisies in the bedroom</u>, thanks for
<u>your many thoughtful kindnesses</u>.

Sometimes, the best way to say "thanks" is with a phone call.

KINDNESS

You really know
how to treat a <u>person</u> right.

◦◦

You are <u>awesome cool</u>
to be so kind.

◦◦

For your thoughtful kindness
and kind thoughtfulness,
<u>my</u> profound thanks.

◦◦

<u>I'm</u> in total awe at
the <u>care and compassion</u> you've
shown <u>my family and me</u>.

◦◦

A <u>billion</u> thank you's
wouldn't be enough
for your <u>infinite kindness</u>.

Personalizing each thank you note helps show your sincerity and gratitude.

words to the rescue { Thank You

SUPPORT

It wasn't a knight on a
white horse that galloped to <u>my</u> rescue.
It was much better: You.

∽

You've lifted the weight of the world
off <u>my</u> shoulders. Thanks a ton.

∽

Like a wheel spinning in the mud,
everyone gets stuck now and then.
Thanks for the push.

∽

Your outpouring of <u>love</u> and <u>compassion</u>
has touched <u>us</u> in a way we'll never forget.

∽

Some people have a natural way of knowing how
to support others. You're one of them.

Put something amazing in a friend's mailbox. Send a thank you card.

words to the rescue ⸚ Thank You

WEDDING

Your presence at our wedding
was the best present.

❧

Thanks for your generous $100 wedding gift.
Jack and I vow to use it wisely.

❧

Props, accolades and hugs from two caffeine
junkies. We love the cappuccino maker.

❧

One of life's joys is gathering around the
table with loved ones. The beautiful china you
gave us will be part of many special occasions.

❧

How generous of you to help us start
our life together with $250. We're saving for
a new kitchen, so it's greatly appreciated.

Have 100 thank you notes to write? Complete ten each day for ten days.

Thank You

WEDDING

You made <u>us</u> feel like royalty.

❧

All <u>we</u> can say is <u>fantastic</u>...
<u>five stars</u>... and most of all, thanks.

❧

Many words say "thank you."
But none seem sufficient to say
how much <u>we</u> appreciate the <u>new car</u>.

❧

I'm picturing a sunny day,
<u>Ross and me</u> hopping in the car,
your <u>beautiful picnic basket</u> in tow.

❧

The <u>cookware set</u> is out of this world.
But that's no surprise from <u>friends</u>
who mean the world to us.

See Fast Phrases, page 141, for more Thank You ideas.

9.
Thinking of You

If I had a single flower for every time I think about you,
I could walk forever in my garden.

~ Claudia Ghandi

My think tank is filled
with thoughts of you.

⌒

While I can't be there
close to you, my thoughts are.

⌒

Thinking of you doesn't just rock
my brainwaves, it creates a tsunami.

⌒

Every waking moment and every one asleep,
thoughts of you I forever keep.

To personalize a message, insert your own words where underlines appear.

Thinking of You

If I thought of you any more,
my skull would burst.

❧

Thinking of you is easy.
It's being apart that's hard.

❧

You keep _me_ in stitches. You keep _me_ on
_my_ toes. That's why _I_ keep thinking of you.

❧

My mind is fixated on one thing lately.
Bear hugging you.

❧

Imagine me as Rodin's "The Thinker."
Above my head is a heart-shaped
bubble with a picture of you.

Not sure what to say? Just write "Thinking of you fondly." That says it all.

{ Thinking of You

Thinking of you, my chickadee.

∽

It's easy for my mind to obsess...
when the one I'm obsessing about is you.

∽

All day long, all I can manage to think
about is you. (No wonder I'm so happy.)

∽

Inky dinky do... just thinking of you.

∽

There's only one reason for this message...
to get you to crack a smile. Come on now. There
you go. Doesn't it feel good?

Keep blank note cards in your desk so it's easy to write a quick note.

Thinking of You

The very thought of your face
puts a smile on <u>mine/ours</u>.

❧

There are lots of us
sending you lots of good thoughts.

❧

You are never far from my thoughts.
(Never more than half an inch, I promise.)

❧

Get your grin on, <u>Elise</u>. You're being
thought of fondly this very moment.

❧

<u>We're</u> not worried about you.
<u>We're</u> just trying to channel our concern
as creatively as possible.

Remember to check this chapter for Sympathy and Encouragement notes.

10.
Valentine's Day

Love is the flower you've got to let grow.

~ John Lennon

Your wish. <u>My</u> command.

Warning: Cupid has an extra arrow.
It's pointed at you.

Warning: Cupid has an extra arrow.
It's pointed at you.

I just bought some track shoes for
my heart. It has a new hobby... racing.

If you see me wearing an oxygen mask,
don't be shocked. The more I know you,
the more you take my breath away.

To personalize a message, insert your own words where <u>underlines</u> appear.

Valentine's Day

FRIENDS

Valentine, we were M-F-E-O:
Made For Each Other.

❧

Happy, happy to my
silly-willy-vanilly Valentine.

❧

To my rock star Valentine...
nobody jams like you.

❧

I love you as big as
a <u>Tyrannosaurus Rex</u>.

❧

Wishing you a big red heart, a hug,
a kiss, a wink, a smile... total bliss.

Love notes don't have to be serious. Try silly, humorous and fun words.

FRIENDS

Consider me 100%
officially captivated.

∽

Valentine, you rock
my city block.

∽

Your heart's in the right place,
Valentine... right next to mine.

∽

Happy "Big V Day" to my very <u>kind</u>,
very <u>talented</u>, very <u>funny</u> <u>housemate</u>.

∽

Valentine: You're a little <u>crazy</u>,
a little <u>demented</u>, and a LOT of fun.

There are many ways to express your love. Do what's comfortable for you.

TO HIM

To the man with
a beautiful heart... a beautiful smile...
and a beautiful everything.

∽

Brad: You have just confirmed my
suspicions. I may very well be
the luckiest woman alive.

∽

The shelter I find in your arms
is like being in a log home built
with sturdy redwoods.

∽

To the funny guy who makes me
laugh, even when he's not trying.

∽

You're stronger than a Texas steer
and hotter than 5-alarm chili.

Surprise him: Stick a Valentine's Day note on the dashboard of his car.

Valentine's Day

TO HER

Happy Cupid Day to my
BHM: Beautiful Hot Mama.

∽

To the <u>wise woman</u> who
taught me the meaning of "wife."

∽

Your hubster loves ya more
today than ever before.

∽

To my <u>Champagne Lady</u>:
You may be the <u>toast of Chicago</u>
but, lucky me, you're all mine.

∽

According to the Bible,
Solomon had 1,000 wives. But
just one is all I'll ever need... YOU.

For more ideas, see the Romance & Fun chapter, page 69.

Valentine's Day

PARTNERS

I now know my place
in life. It's with you.

∽

Happiness happens...
and it's happening to me.

∽

It's impossible to spell
MARVELOUS without US.

∽

If you believe for one minute
I'm the kind of Valentine that responds
to gratuitous flattery... you're right.

∽

Life is a lazy river. Let's float
down it together in purple inner tubes.

Slip a Valentine note in your spouse's purse or briefcase.

PARTNERS

I need a favor, Valentine.
Would you please try not to be
<u>so charming</u>? You're killing me.

Did anyone ever tell you, you have
the best DNA? (Darn Nice Assets)

After all these years,
I don't see how it would be possible
<u>to love you any more</u> than I do.

Life without you, my little burrito,
is like rice without beans.

Remember the scene in the *Wizard of Oz*,
when everything changed from black and
white to color? That's my life with you.

Tired of the same old thing? Celebrate Valentine's Day a day early.

Valentine's Day

PARTNERS

Let's spend <u>Saturday</u> together
doing a whole lot of nothin'.

❧

I'd love to learn to <u>Tango</u>.
You game, Valentine?

❧

Happy "Big V Day" to
my big cuddly teddy bear.

❧

Know what's weird Valentine?
You have this way of making me <u>insane</u>.
Yet I'll always be <u>crazy</u> about you.

❧

Note to co-pilot: My biggest wish
is to be in a holding pattern with you.

Instead of a Valentine's card, leave a note on the bathroom mirror.

11.
Easter

The story of Easter is the story of
God's wonderful window of divine surprise.
~ Carl Knudsen

Joy shines today,
brightly, infinitely.

Easter wishes... springtime kisses.

Baskets of Easter blessings to
our <u>lovely neighbor,</u> <u>Mrs. Farina</u>.

Boing, boing, boing, spring has sprung.
A blooming good Easter to everyone.

To personalize a message, insert your own words where <u>underlines</u> appear.

RELIGIOUS

May the light of the risen Christ
shine for you.

∽◦

God's grace to you on this joyous day,
the cornerstone of our Christian faith.

∽◦

Easter is hope. On this profound day, God
shows us that life doesn't end with death.

∽◦

Our Lord has written the promise
of resurrection, not in books alone,
but in every leaf of springtime.
~ Martin Luther

∽◦

Christ's death and resurrection
changed everything. May the
Easter miracle change each of us.

Celebrate the joy of Easter. Let loved ones know you appreciate them.

Easter

GENERAL

Happy Easter, buddy.

⚮

Easter greetings to the
most colorful egg in the bunch.

⚮

Wishing you the rich
blessings of the Easter season.

⚮

Jelly beans and Easter bonnets,
glazed ham with pineapple on it,
colored eggs and chocolate bunnies,
love to you this Easter, honey.

⚮

Spring... and the earth
awakens, joyfully, colorfully,
affirming the seasons of life.

Easter is from "Eostre," an ancient Anglo-Saxon goddess, symbolized by the egg.

words to the rescue ⎰ **Easter**

Peace, love
and jelly beans.

⌒

Wishing you the glow
of a spring rainbow.

⌒

Yellow daffodils and smiles
to <u>my favorite teacher</u> on Easter.

⌒

Blooms, butterflies and blessings
to you this happy season.

⌒

Spring is here. Baseball is back.
Life is good. Let's tip a beer
to our favorite time of year.

Use this book to help you write clever Facebook messages throughout the year.

12.
Mother's Day

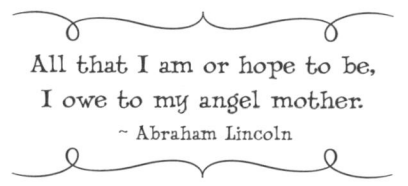

All that I am or hope to be,
I owe to my angel mother.
~ Abraham Lincoln

Mom, you're the best.
Magnificent. Outstanding.
Marvelous.

∽◦

To my domestic goddess
on Mother's Day, Love Zeus.

∽◦

Today we're screaming your
praises: Mom, you're a rock star.

∽◦

Happy Mother's Day to the lady
we love for all you do and all you are.

To personalize a message, insert your own words where <u>underlines</u> appear.

Thank you, Mom, for raising me
to be <u>the human being I am today</u>.

❧

To the new mommy who's
doing a heck of a job.

❧

Even when it looked like I was
wilting, you kept on shining for me, Mom.
Love and thanks from your flower child.

❧

You should be treated like royalty.
With a crowning achievement like
<u>our family/me</u>, you deserve the world.

❧

Mom, without you, I don't know how we
would have made it through <u>the rough times</u>.

Share a fun memory from your childhood. Your mom will get a kick out of it.

To an absolutely Mom-tastic mom.

❧

Remembering <u>the fun times</u> when
<u>you and Dad took us all to the cottage.</u>

❧

We've had our ups and downs.
But, Mom, you'll always have a special
place in my heart.

❧

Thanks, Mom, for showing me the way. The
way to <u>iron a shirt...</u> the way to <u>fry chicken...</u>
and mostly, the way to <u>live a good life.</u>

❧

Who's faster than a speeding minivan, more
powerful than a cyclonic vacuum and can leap
over loads of laundry in a single bound?

Pick three positive character traits about your mom; include them in a note.

Hugs and kisses to the
mom with a heart as big as <u>Miami</u>.

✑

The Pope called.
He said you've been approved
for sainthood. It's about time.

✑

Momma... we love you more than
ice cream and pink cotton candy combined.

✑

Mom, you've done real good.
You raised the bar on raising kids.

✑

As you show us gently every day,
Motherhood is the highest calling.

Haven't spoken to mom in awhile? Break the ice with a Mother's Day note.

108

13.
Father's Day

A father's words are like a thermostat that
sets the temperature in the house.

~ Paul Lewis

Yesterday a dude; today a dad.

It's a bird. It's a plane.
No, it's Super Dad.
(Thanks for being our hero.)

Props to you, Dad.
You're the engine that
keeps our family flying high.

Lucky, lucky <u>me</u>
to have a father as <u>fun</u> as you.

To personalize a message, insert your own words where <u>underlines</u> appear.

Father's Day

It's true: Good things
come in TALL packages.

～

Dad: Your <u>strong moral character</u>
and <u>firm, loving guidance</u> is
the foundation of our family.

～

"Well done" describes a steak. It also
describes the job you do as our Dad.

～

It's humanly impossible to be a perfect
Dad. But who said you're a mere mortal?

～

To the best dad ever, who always <u>plays
catch with me</u> and <u>buys me gummy worms.</u>

Dads give lots of pats on the back. This is the time to give him one in return.

⟨ **Father's Day**

Whoa, Daddy-O.

❧

You're the <u>smartest</u>, <u>nicest</u>
and <u>most caring</u> Dad a kid could have.

❧

Dedicated. Awesome. Definitely cool.
D.A.D. you're a stand out.

❧

We hereby proclaim you "Dad of
the Year." (We'll skip the crown
and sash in favor of a hug and kiss.)

❧

Know what I just realized?
The dad you were to me has helped
me be a better dad to my kids.

Give dad a note listing three ways you're a better person because of him.

Pops, you're tops.

☙

You're not an ordinary Dad,
not run-of-the-mill. We love
spending time with you just to chill.

☙

<u>We</u> salute you, Dad, for being
the <u>kick-ass</u> captain of our family.

☙

Dad: You may be a <u>geek</u>.
But you're our own special <u>geek</u>
who we love <u>megabytes</u>.

☙

Dad, thank you for <u>caring about me so much</u>.
I don't know who else in this world would
<u>stick up for me</u> like you do.

Think of three positive words that describe your dad. Share them in a note.

14.
Thanksgiving

Not what we say about our blessings, but how we use
them, is the true measure of our thanksgiving.
~ W.T. Purkiser

We take our
Pilgrim's hats off to you.

A cornucopia of thanks for
all the ways you make life sweeter.

For health. For home.
For family. For you.

The best things in life aren't things.
Today we give thanks for them.

To personalize a message, insert your own words where <u>underlines</u> appear.

Thanksgiving

A rushing river of gratitude
is flowing your way.

∽

This season of gratitude, we're
shining the spotlight on you
for all you've done and all you do.

∽

Mom and Dad, you give us much to be
thankful for. Especially your good hearts.

∽

On this feast of counting blessings,
your <u>hostess</u> politely requests:
Please do not count the calories.

∽

Twenty-one salutes. Three cheers. And
one big hoo-ah for <u>our Thanksgiving hosts</u>.

Expressing gratitude is healthy. It makes everyone feel good.

This <u>Thanksgiving</u>,
we are rich. We have <u>each other</u>.

⌒

Thanksgiving <u>cheer</u> to a <u>man</u> who
makes others happy all year long.

⌒

The intensity of <u>our</u> gratitude
is matched only by the strength
of <u>our</u> love for you, <u>Mom and Dad</u>.

⌒

In this big wonderful world, many people
deserve <u>our</u> thanks. Especially you.

⌒

As we reflect on the prosperity we enjoy
as Americans, let us also commit to sharing
our resources with others less fortunate.

For more ways to thank others, see Fast Phrases, page 141.

We're <u>crazy lucky</u>
to live in this country.

⤴

Heartfelt grins... soul-felt gratitude.

⤴

Your support, both as <u>a business partner</u> and
<u>a friend</u>, is genuinely appreciated, not only at
this time of gratitude but throughout the year.

⤴

Your ongoing support is an
<u>unending blessing</u> to all of us at
<u>Excel Academy</u>. Our <u>infinite</u> thanks.

⤴

For you, <u>Pastor Ellen</u>, the dedicated
leader you are, and the better human beings
you inspire us to be, we say, "Thanks."

Forget to send a thank you note? It's never too late. Do it today.

15.
Christmas

Every time we love, every time we give,
it's Christmas. ~ Dale Evans

Rock it out, Santa baby.

Give <u>everyone</u> a super big
Santa squeeze for <u>us</u>.

Seasonal tip for busy <u>moms</u>:
Take time to enjoy. Take naps.

Of the six billion people on earth, there's only
one I want to spend Christmas with: <u>You</u>.

To personalize a message, insert your own words where <u>underlines</u> appear.

Christmas without you is like
a candy cane without stripes.

❧

Thinking of you lovingly this holiday.

❧

Christmas is when God came down
from heaven with a baby in His arms.

~ R. Eugene Sterner

❧

Good friends. Good talk. Good food.
Please join us for a rockin' good time.

❧

Rituals are comforting, especially
in times of uncertainty. I hope you revel
in <u>our family gatherings</u> as much as I do.

Writing holiday thank you cards? See the Thank You chapter, page 81.

Christmas

Santa says...
do something nice for a stranger.

∽↫

Come all ye faithful... and all ye
who love to party at the <u>Jones'</u>.

∽↫

Irish you a Merry Christmas,
and a lucky leprechaun New Year.

∽↫

No matter how many places I travel,
there's still snow place like home.

∽↫

This has been a hard year
for all of us. How good it will be
to be together for Christmas.

Add fun to Christmas cards. Decorate the envelopes with colored markers.

Mix things up a bit.
Have yourself a
varied Merry Christmas.

◦◦

Joy to the world!
But most of all, to <u>the Lawtons</u>.

◦◦

May you be touched by the
wonder of earth and sky and the
majesty of God's creation.

◦◦

The wise men had it right. May you too
follow wherever the star leads.

◦◦

<u>My</u> wish for you: Bright stars, joyous songs
and warm chats by stone fireplaces.

Make a personalized holiday card featuring your favorite family photos.

This Christmas, think green...
kiss someone Irish.

❧

May God abundantly bless us
this Christmas, and keep our old
bones healthy throughout the year.

❧

This cheerful season, may <u>peace</u> fill
your home, and <u>tequila</u> fill your glass.

❧

<u>Pastor:</u> You've been a beacon of light to us.
May your holidays shine as brightly as you.

❧

Experts say you can pack on
ten pounds this time of year. I say, bring on
the red-sprinkled star-shaped sugar cookies.

Too busy to send Christmas cards? Send Happy New Year cards instead.

It's tinsel time...
glitz and glam time.

༄

Some things in life really matter.
This is the time of year
we unabashedly celebrate them.

༄

Happy snowflakes.
Happy fruitcakes. Happy reindeer games.

༄

Life overflows with goodness.
Enjoy as much of it as possible.

༄

I'll always remember <u>Aunt Mary's
cherry tarts</u>... and <u>how she lovingly
whipped every lump out of the turkey gravy.</u>

Holiday gathering game: Players guess what years famiy photos were taken.

Warm wishes
to <u>wonderful neighbors</u>.

⸎

Kids are the bright lights of the season.
You've raised some <u>awesome</u> ones.

⸎

This season, make a special effort
to discover the joy of <u>community</u>.

⸎

Christmas blessings to <u>Marcus, Destiny and
Owen</u>, three <u>sweet munchkins</u> with two
parents that aren't half bad either.

⸎

We'll always treasure Christmas memories
<u>living next to the Joneses</u>. Remember when
<u>Jimmy and Ally dressed up as elves</u>?

Post holiday signs in your home like "Welcome Smiths." Watch guests smile.

Jingles, my friend.

⌾

A hot chocolate holiday
to you.

⌾

Though times have been rough,
our Christmas spirit is still shining.

⌾

Let's celebrate candy canes, church
traditions, the love of family, the cheer
of friends and <u>love</u> that never ends.

⌾

The purity of fallen snow... the silence of a
star-filled night... the fragrance of a freshly-
cut pine. This holiday, savor the simple things.

Do a nice thing. Send holiday cards to military personnel stationed overseas.

16.
New Year

Happy **YOU** year!

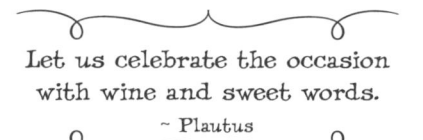

A new year is an open sky
of possibilities. May you soar.

Magnificent things are ahead
for you. My crystal ball said so.

If last year was a <u>roller coaster</u>,
this one's going to be a <u>merry-go-round</u>.
Watch and see.

To personalize a message, insert your own words where <u>underlines</u> appear.

How grateful I am that we
<u>reconnected on Facebook</u> this year.

∽

Good <u>food</u>... good <u>talk</u>... good <u>tunes</u>.
Good thing I've got you <u>for a friend</u>.

∽

There is just one thing I ask of you
this year. To enjoy <u>insane happiness</u>.

∽

If you think for one minute we're
going to be happy this year, you're wrong.
We're going to be <u>freaking ecstatic</u>.

∽

Open new doors... travel new roads...
taste new flavors. Your life will be <u>richer</u>.

Use this time of year to plan your success strategy for the coming 365 days.

This year, take a chance.
Dance.

∽

Wishing you a year filled with <u>roaring
laughter</u>, <u>crazy joy</u> and <u>unlimited hot coffee</u>.

∽

Fitness, fabulousness and a fiercely
good year to my <u>partner in crime</u>.

∽

Recipe for a delicious year:
Everything tastes better with <u>bacon</u>.

∽

First you take a drink, then the drink
takes a drink, then the drink takes you.

~ F. Scott Fitzgerald

Think of three people who made last year easier for you. Write to them.

words to the rescue 〉 New Year

<u>We're</u> dubbing this year,
"The year of <u>Jessica</u>."

∽

Good resolutions are like babies
crying in church. They should be
carried out immediately.
~ Charles M. Sheldon

∽

My wish for you: Everything positive...
everything wise... everything beautiful...
and infinite blue skies.

∽

Destiny is not a matter of chance;
it is a matter of choice.
~ Author Unknown

∽

Nothing but the best to a <u>guy</u> who deserves it.

Wrap up the year by telling a friend how much you appreciate them.

Failure is the opportunity
to begin again more intelligently.
~ Henry Ford

⌒

Better health... better times... better year.

⌒

Let's party. Let's do it up big.
It's a whole new beginning...
a brand new gig.

⌒

A new year is like a clean,
white sheet of paper.
What story do you want to write?

⌒

Smooth sailing. Oceans of good luck.
Happy New Year, mate.

Set a goal to keep in touch more often with the important people in your life.

Applaud us when we run. Console us
when we fall. Cheer us when we recover.
~ Edmund Burke

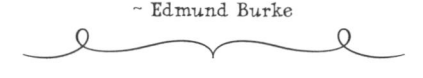

Fast Phrases

Need maximum inspiration in
minimum time? Scan these pages. Like
fireworks for your brain, Fast Phrases
gives you hundreds of ideas to spark
your writing creativity.

> The years teach much which
> the days never knew.
> ~ Ralph Waldo Emerson

fast phrases 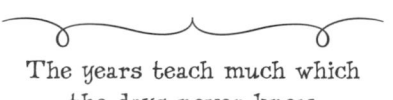 **Birthday**

A wish to a wise soul

Aging splendidly I see

Bam bam birthday man

Balloons for a big baboon

Birthday bliss-out

Birthday embraces

Celebrate the bad boy

Cheese and cracker time

Cheers for the young stud

Confetti time

Crank up the volume

Destined for diva-hood

Go fried bananas

Have a boffo birthday

Infinite rainbows

Fireworks from your #1 fan

Glory, glitz and glam, ma'am

Hippie Birthday, my hippie

Ice cream all around

Kudos, commander

Let's bash this birthday

Make merry, Mary

Make noise for...

Oldsters know best

One year bolder

On this solemn day

Our elder statesman

Party hearty

Peace out, papa

Pig out on joy

Screaming ice cream

Shine on supa-sta

Smokin' hot

Splendiferous day

Shake, rattle and roll

Seize the birthday

Still standing strong

Sunshine sister

Terrible 2's

Twinkle toes forever

Kind words will unlock an iron door.
~ Turkish proverb

fast phrases ∫ Congratulations

7 salutes to 7 talented girls
A fearless, fantastic feat
Accolades, oh mighty one
Bask in the spotlight
Bravo, babycakes
Bumpy road to success
Champions over all
Clap, cheer, have a beer
Congrats x 100
Display of excellence
Feather in your fedora
Good stuff, you guys
Grade "A" performance
Great for you
Infinite accolades
Kudos, kids
Man, you're good
Mr. Tour de Force
Ms. Ultra-Talented
One word: Astonishing

Our highest praise
Persistence pays
Take your victory lap
Talent always prevails
To my triumphant teen
To the top dogs
Top of the mountain
Victory time, baby
We're totally psyched
What a masterstroke
Way to go, winners
You delivered, baby
You came through
You dominated
You made it happen
You rocked the stage
Your genius is showing
Well deserved win
We're dang proud
Winner's circle time

Better than a thousand hollow words
is one word that brings peace.
~ Buddha

fast phrases ⎰ Christmas

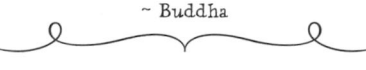

Adventures in shopping	Joy filled munchkins
All roads lead home	Let the festivities begin
Boughs of joy	Light up the night
Celebrate the savior	Magical time of year
Cheer far and near	Ornamental moments
Chocolate memories	Peace-out party
Choirs of angels	Put your feet up
Christmas craziness	Peppermint kisses
Crunch of wrapping paper	Rainbow of lights
Decorating divas	Reindeers rule
Dinner at Grandma's	Signs of St. Nick
Embrace your inner elf	Sing your heart out
Fireside moments	Snowflakes forever
Fruitcake fever	Spread the love
Gather around the tree	Stockings on the mantel
Gifts all around	Treasured traditions
Give it up for Baby Jesus	Twinkling hearts
Hearts connected	Warmth of friendship
Holiday houses aglow	Wrapped with love
Hot cocoa for all	Yuletide Yummies

> If you want others to be happy, practice compassion.
> If you want to be happy, practice compassion.
> ~ Dalai Lama

fast phrases  Dedicated To...

A divine friend	Fishing, family & friends
A fantastic father	Flying sky high
A magnificent mom	Fun new projects
A mechanic with drive	Giving second chances
A joyful marriage	Global adventures
A musician of note	Lazy, crazy weekends
A pastor with soul	Never saying never
A teacher with class	Nothing but net
A trainer with muscle	Our best year ever
All God's creatures	Putting your feet up
All things wild	Roads not yet taken
Amazing animal friends	Seizing opportunities
An upper-crust baker	Sharing wisdom
Barefoot beach days	Success in excess
Barrels of fun	Talent and teamwork
Bold originals	The best kids ever
Busting the budget	The power of faith
Crazy city nights	Unwavering faith
Everlasting love	Vintage vibes
Everything pink	Winding, bumpy roads

One joy scatters a hundred griefs.
~ Chinese Proverb

fast phrases  Encouragement

A heartfelt hoorah
Always a winner
Charge ahead
Cherishing you
Dig down deep
Everyone needs a boost
Give it your best shot
Fighting spirit
Friends you can turn to
Family to boost you
Hugs across the miles
I understand it's difficult
I'm here to lift you up
I know you have it
Keep fighting for it
Lean on me whenever
My rally cry for you
May success be yours
Never back down
Powerful moments in life

Praying for success
Rely on inner strength
Supporting the cause
Things will get better
This one's for you
The power of faith
We'll work this out
We're rooting for you
We believe in you
We're on your side
We think of you often
We've got your back
We're here to push you
You gave it your all
Your support squad
You've got the goods
You are important to us
You are sooo loved
You've got this, kiddo

Poetry: The best words in the best order.
~ Samuel Taylor Coleridge

fast phrases) **Exclamations**

Attaboy

Awesome-tastic

Dear me

Freaking fabulous

Freaking fantastic

Gadzooks

Gee whillikers

Gracious me

Golly gee

Goosebump city

Heavens to Betsy

Here here

Hey hey hey

Holy angel wings

Holy biker chic

Holy canoli

Holy cow

Holy moly

Jeepers creepers

Mama mia

Mercy mercy me

My stars

Oh fiddlesticks

Okey-dokey

Presto

Sakes alive

Sha-ZAM

Sheesh

Shiver me timbers

Well gol-lee me

What a hoot

What a surprise

What a joy

Whooo-hooo

Whoa

Whoop-de-do

Wowie zowie

Yippee do da day

Yoo-hoo

fast phrases  Get Well

Amazing doctors	Heartfelt prayers
Attitude of healing	I understand
Back in the pink	I know it hurts
Back in the saddle	Keep the faith
Bandage the hurt	Keep your positive spirit
Be healthy and happy	Mind your meds
Be good to yourself	Nurses know best
Better than new	On your feet again
Blessings and bear hugs	Out of the woods
Bright and bushy-tailed	On your way back
Comforting thoughts	Pamper yourself
Care package for you	Praying for miracles
Ease the pain	Process of healing
Eat apples daily	Rest and relax
Emotional healing	Renewed vitality
Feeling great again	Sending caring thoughts
Flourishing health	Stay positive and strong
Get fit and fabulous	Thank God you made it
Grateful for you	Your old chipper self
Harmony and health	Your soul is strong
Healing environment	A wish for your health

> Let us be grateful to people who make us happy; they are
> the charming gardeners who make our souls blossom.
> ~ Marcel Proust

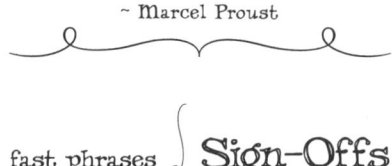

fast phrases ⟩ ## Sign-Offs

Arrivederci	Rock it out
Buenas noches	Stay beautiful
C-ya	Stay cool
Catch ya later	Stay young
Cheerio	Tallyho
Forever yours	Ten-four
G'day	Thanks a million
Guten tag	To your health
Keep on truckin'	To your success
Keep being you	Until next time
Keep laughing	Warmly yours
Keep out of trouble	With a glad heart
Keep stretching	With a heavy heart
Later 'gator	With bear hugs
Never look back	With bountiful blessings
Obsessively yours	With fond thoughts
Over and out	With greatest respect
Prayerful best wishes	With love & laughs
Prayers & hugs	With passion & purpose
Peace out	With sincere gratitude

What is required is not a lot of words
but effectual ones.

~ Seneca

fast phrases 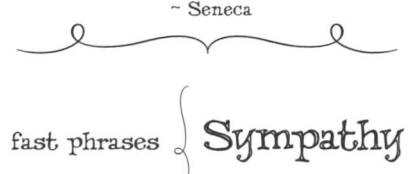 Sympathy

At this sad time
Can't find words
Can't imagine the pain
Close in our thoughts
Courage and strength
Comfort in God's grace
Crying for you
Dearly missed
Deeply sorry
Difficult days
Enormous loss
Farewell, friend
God's gentle peace
Gone too soon
Hard to say goodbye
Heartbroken to pieces
Hearts are sad
Her light shines on
Hole in my heart
Honored to have known

Honoring his life
Hurting so bad
I'll always remember
Left us too soon
Legacy of love
Love and sympathy
Love and hugs
Love and support
Lifetime of memories
Live in our memories
May you find solace
Many condolences
Memories live on
Mourning with you
My deep respect
My heart is aching
Never forgotten
Prayerfully
Sadly we say farewell
We're here for you

A thankful heart is not only the greatest virtue
but the parent of all other virtues.

~ Cicero

fast phrases 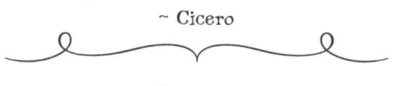 Thank You

A gift to remember
A river of thanks
Amazing gift of love
An honor and delight
Appreciation acclamation
Awed by generosity
Baskets of thanks
Blown away by it all
Cheers to the pioneers
Couldn't be more pleased
Danke... gracias... merci
Elated by your gift
Extremely gratifying
Forever grateful
How apropos
Indebted to you
Just what we need
Kindness beyond words
Lifted our spirits
Meaningful moments

Much obliged
Mammoth thanks
Mucho mucho thanks
Not all gifts come in boxes
Out of this universe
Our most sincere gratitude
So darn thoughtful
Soulfelt gratitude
Thanks a bushel
Thanks a ton and a half
Thunderous applause
Touched my heart
Uplifted by your kindness
What a total surprise
We reverently bow
You deserve our praise
You're one great dude
Your gift was spot on
We owe you big time
We'll be forever smiling

> Be glad of life, because it gives you the chance to love
> and work, to play and to look up at the stars.
> – Henry Van Dyke

fast phrases ⟩ Wishes

Happy...
...travels & trails
...moving ahead day
...yoga poses
...cave exploring
...new adventures
...final exams
...dog walking
...treasure hunting
...celebrity seeking
...storm chasing
...diamond shopping
...UFO sightings
...shower singing
...raspberry lemonade
...belly laughs
...moon dances
...library lounging
...downtown delights

Hugs, kisses and...
...graduation wishes
...lots of fishes
...scrumptuous dishes

Long live...
...anti-depressants
...cappuccino grandes
...college football buds
...cool cats with rhythm
...poppy seed bagels
...steam saunas
...double margaritas
...tigers, lions and bears

May your...
...iPad never crash
...days be decadently fun
...travels intoxicate you
...shoes always shine
...hair always obey

> Personality has the power to open many doors.
> But character must keep them open.
> ~ Author unknown

Personality Picks

When you need a quick personal message,
scan the following pages. Pick one or more
of the positive personality traits that fit
the person you are writing to or about.
Finally, place them in a sentence appropriate
to the occasion, like the example below.

Example:

Congratulations, my intelligent,
organized and outrageous friend, on
your graduation from medical school.

Goodness is the only investment that never fails.
~ Henry David Thoreau

words to the rescue  **Personality Picks**

Able	Brave	Connected
Accomplished	Bright	Congenial
Admirable	Brilliant	Contemporary
Affectionate	Capable	Courageous
Aggressive	Caring	Conscientious
Animated	Calm	Creative
Adventurous	Candid	Curious
Altruistic	Careful	Decisive
Amiable	Casual	Debonair
Analytical	Charming	Dedicated
Approachable	Clever	Determined
Athletic	Charismatic	Diligent
Artistic	Cheerful	Disciplined
Artful	Coordinated	Distinguished
Attentive	Compassionate	Direct
Authoritative	Committed	Driven
Avant Garde	Comedic	Easygoing
Beautiful	Comical	Eccentric
Buttoned-up	Communicative	Educated
Blunt	Competitive	Effective
Bodacious	Composed	Eloquent

> Try not to become a man of success
> but rather try to become a man of value.
> ~ Albert Einstein

words to the rescue **Personality Picks**

Empathetic	Genuine	Inquisitive
Encouraging	Giddy	Joyful
Energetic	Gifted	Jovial
Engaging	Gracious	Kind
Esoteric	Grateful	Light-hearted
Exacting	Gregarious	Likeable
Excited	Hands-on	Logical
Expressive	Handsome	Loving
Exuberant	Hard-working	Lovely
Fashionable	Helpful	Loyal
Fanatical	Hilarious	Low-key
Fearless	Humorous	Magical
Focused	Humble	Mature
Forceful	Imaginative	Methodical
Frank	Impulsive	Meticulous
Friendly	Independent	Mechanical
Funny	Industrious	Moral
Fun-loving	Innocent	Musical
Generous	Intelligent	Mysterious
Genius	Inspired	Neat
Gentle	Intrepid	Neighborly

> Though we travel the world over to find the beautiful,
> we must carry it within us or we find it not.
> ~ Ralph Waldo Emerson

words to the rescue **Personality Picks**

Nice	Professional	Sensitive
Notorious	Proud	Serene
Opinionated	Quiet	Sexy
Old school	Quick-witted	Sincere
One-of-a-kind	Rare	Skilled
Open	Relentless	Smart
Organized	Religious	Sociable
Outrageous	Renowned	Spirited
Patient	Resourceful	Spirit-filled
Passionate	Resilient	Spiritual
Persuasive	Respectful	Soft-spoken
Persistent	Responsible	Sophisticated
Personable	Rational	Strategic
Physical	Rhythmic	Strong
Polite	Robust	Studious
Popular	Romantic	Stunning
Positive	Safe	Stylish
Prepared	Saucy	Suave
Prestigious	Scientific	Sweet
Proactive	Selfless	Successful
Problem-solver	Self-motivated	Supportive

> Wisdom is oftentimes nearer
> when we stoop than when we soar.
> ~ William Wordsworth

words to the rescue | # Personality Picks

Take charge	Versatile
Talented	Vigorous
Talkative	Vital
Tasteful	Vivacious
Technical	Wacky
Tenacious	Warm
Thankful	Warm-hearted
Thorough	Welcoming
Thoughtful	Well-mannered
Thrifty	Whimsical
Tireless	Winsome
Tolerant	Wise
Trustworthy	Witty
Uncompromising	
Understanding	
Unique	
Unforgettable	
Unmatched	
Unselfish	
Upbeat	
Uplifting	

Meet the Author

 Steve Fadie is an author, publisher, speaker, advertising writer and expert on using minimum words to create maximum impact. The author of *Words to the Rescue*, *Words to the Rescue 2*, and founder of Orange Sky Books, he started making greeting cards at age five.

His passion for words lead to a degree in Communications at Michigan State University and a successful career as an advertising writer. Among his creative endeavors: creating and marketing a line of greeting cards, coaching public speakers, designing effective retail displays and signage, and operating a profitable e-commerce web site.

A lifelong Michigan resident, Steve Fadie lives happily in Commerce Township, one hour northwest of Detroit, surrounded by an abundance of lakes and trees. An ardent supporter of his home state, he is a fan of HGTV, Native American proverbs, creative people, mint chocolate chip ice cream and his cat Tracer.

Free! "Words of the Week" email from Steve Fadie

To receive timely words of inspiration throughout the year, sign up now for Steve's Words of the Week. www.WordsToTheRescue.com

Do you know anyone who could use a few good words?

- Words for personal notes
- Words for Facebook pages
- Words for email and e-cards
- Words for office greeting cards
- Words for handmade cards
- Words for birthday cakes
- Words for toasts
- Words for shout-outs
- Words for lunch box notes
- Words for scrapbook pages
- Words for gift inscriptions
- Words for floral enclosure cards

Give a gift they'll use all year.

To purchase copies of *Words to the Rescue*

and *Words to the Rescue 2,* visit

www.WordsToTheRescue.com

My sincere thanks...

To everyone who helped push, produce and proofread this book.

Thank you to content contributors, including Cheryl Cavender; Mary Fadie; Kathleen Ferres; Kathy Hyink; Patty Kenney; Marlene Kinney; Cheryl Poole; and Joy Wright.

My appreciation to those who reviewed rough drafts, manuscripts and covers, including Carol Arnosky, Scrapbooks Galore and More, Midland Michigan; proofreader extraordinaire Peter Artemas; Margene Buckhave, Stamp Peddler Plus, Northville, Michigan; Janine Dailey; Carol Graham; Kathy Hyink; Denise Jacobs; Patty Kenney; Michelle Michael; Gene Romer; Susan White and CJ Wolfe.

Gracias to everyone whose support, big or small, kept this project moving forward, including bagel shop bud Bob Matthews; Michelle Corra, Photo Expressions, Maple Ridge, British Columbia, Canada; Art Director Ilya Hardy; Phyllis Fadie; Anne Marie DeFrain; Kelley and Kevin Poppe, The Scrapbook Zone, Farmington Michigan; Kathy Sheldon and Jim White.

Use these pages to collect favorite words and quotes, to remind yourself of important dates, and to record which messages you sent to whom, so you don't repeat.

Notes:

_____

_____

_____

_____

_____

_____

_____

_____

_____

_____

_____

_____

_____

_____

_____

_____

_____

_____

_____

_____

Notes:

Notes:

Notes

Notes

Words are but air; the pen leaves a mark.
~ Chinese proverb